How Toys Work

T0080566

Screws, Nuts, and Bolts

Siân Smith

Heinemann LIBRARY

Chicago, Illinois

www.capstonepub.com
Visit our website to find out more information about Heinemann-Raintree books.

To order:
☎ Phone 800-747-4992
💻 Visit www.capstonepub.com
to browse our catalog and order online.

© 2013 Heinemann Library
an imprint of Capstone Global Library, LLC
Chicago, Illinois

All rights reserved. No part of this publication may be reproduced or transmitted in any form or by any means, electronic or mechanical, including photocopying, recording, taping, or any information storage and retrieval system, without permission in writing from the publisher.

Edited by Dan Nunn, Rebecca Rissman, and Sian Smith Designed by Joanna Hinton-Malivoire
Picture research by Mica Brancic
Production by Victoria Fitzgerald
Originated by Capstone Global Library Ltd

Library of Congress Cataloging-in-Publication Data Smith, Siân.
  Screws, nuts, and bolts / Siân Smith.
     p. cm.—(How toys work)
  Includes bibliographical references and index.
  ISBN 978-1-4329-6582-2 (hb)—ISBN 978-1-4329-6589-1 (pb) 1. Screws—Juvenile literature. 2. Bolts and nuts—Juvenile literature. 3. Toys—Juvenile literature. I. Title.
  TJ1338.S63 2013
  621.8'82—dc23   2011041311

Acknowledgments
The author and publisher are grateful to the following for permission to reproduce copyright material: © Capstone Global Library Ltd pp.8, 17, 22b (Lord and Leverett); © Capstone Publishers pp.6, 7 main, 9 inset, 9 main, 12, 13, 14, 15, 18, 19, 21, 10 inset, 10 main, 11 inset, 23 top (Karon Dubke); Shutterstock pp. 20, 5 (© Noam Armonn), 7 inset (© HomeStudio), 16 (© sonya etchison), 22a (© Nelstudio), 22c (© John Kasawa), 22d (© Tish1), 23 bottom (© HomeStudio), 23 middle bottom (© Jaroslaw Grudzinski), 23 middle top (© Taurus), 4 bottom left (© studio BM), 4 bottom right (© thirayut), 4 top left (© Piotr Sikora), 4 top right (© Noah Golan).

Cover photograph of toys made out of nuts and bolts reproduced with permission of Shutterstock (© Gary Blakeley). Back cover photograph of a wrench being used on a nut reproduced with permission of © Capstone Publishers (Karon Dubke).

We would like to thank David Harrison, Nancy Harris, Dee Reid, and Diana Bentley for their assistance in the preparation of this book.

Every effort has been made to contact copyright holders of material reproduced in this book. Any omissions will be rectified in subsequent printings if notice is given to the publisher.

All the Internet addresses (URLs) given in this book were valid at the time of going to press. However, due to the dynamic nature of the Internet, some addresses may have changed, or sites may have changed or ceased to exist since publication. While the author and publisher regret any inconvenience this may cause readers, no responsibility for any such changes can be accepted by either the author or the publisher.

Contents

Different Toys

There are many different kinds of toys.

Toys work in different ways.

Screws

screws

Some toys use screws.

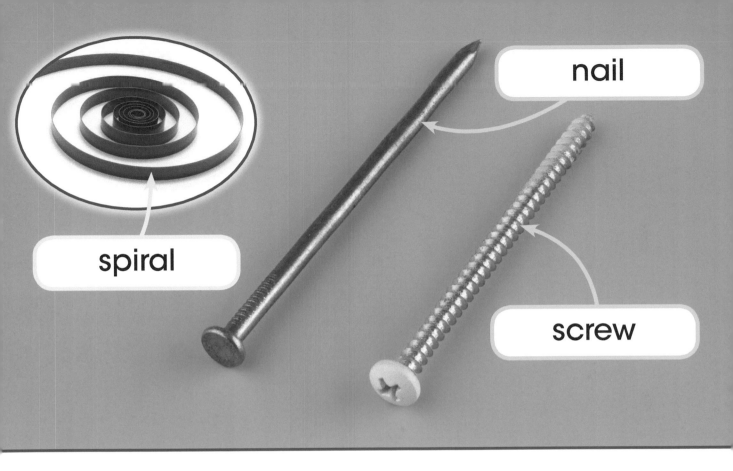

spiral

nail

screw

A screw is like a nail with a spiral wrapped around it.

screw

We use screws to hold things together.

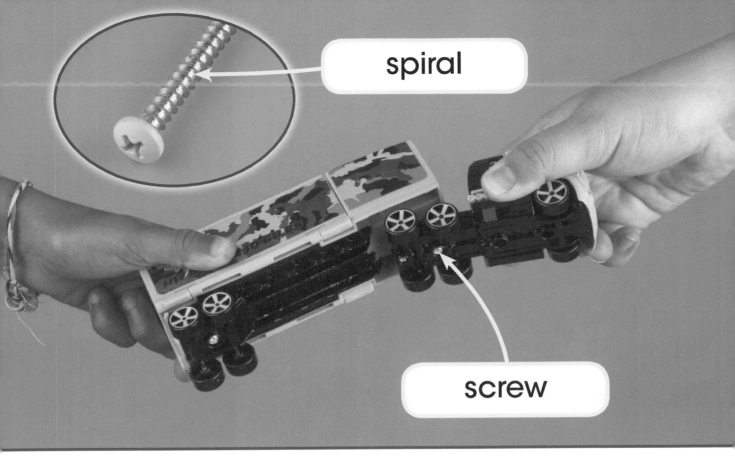

spiral

screw

The spiral on a screw makes it hard to pull out.

Screws hold this car together.

Screws hold this computer game together.

Nuts and Bolts

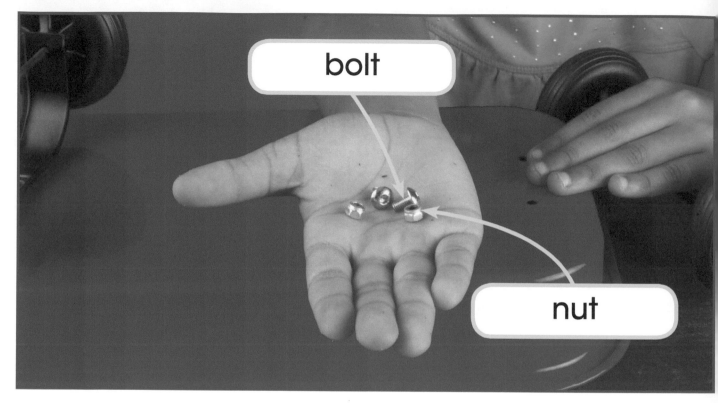

bolt

nut

Some toys use nuts and bolts.

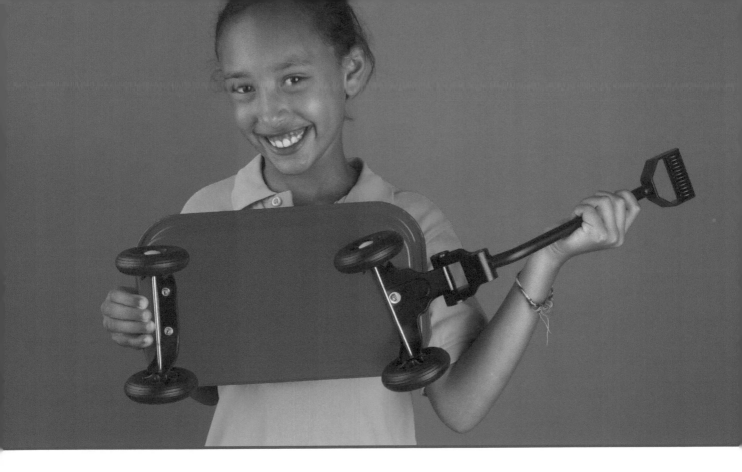

Nuts and bolts hold things together, too.

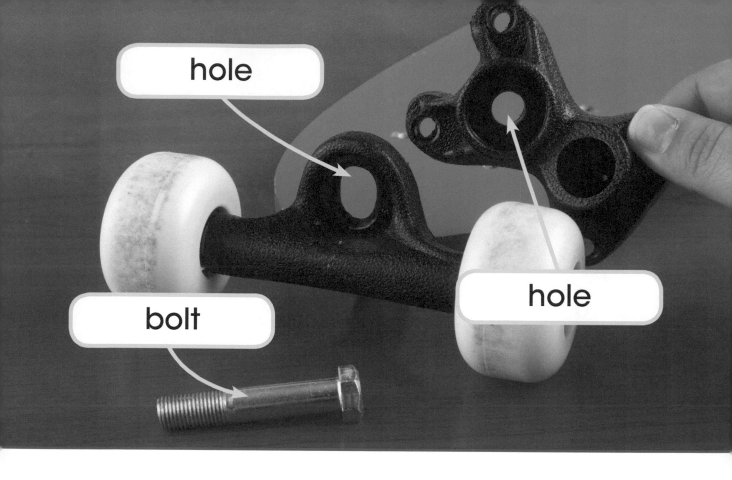

hole

bolt

hole

Two pieces have holes.

A bolt goes through the holes.

nut

A nut goes on the end of the bolt.

It holds the pieces together.

nut and bolt

Nuts and bolts hold this jungle gym together.

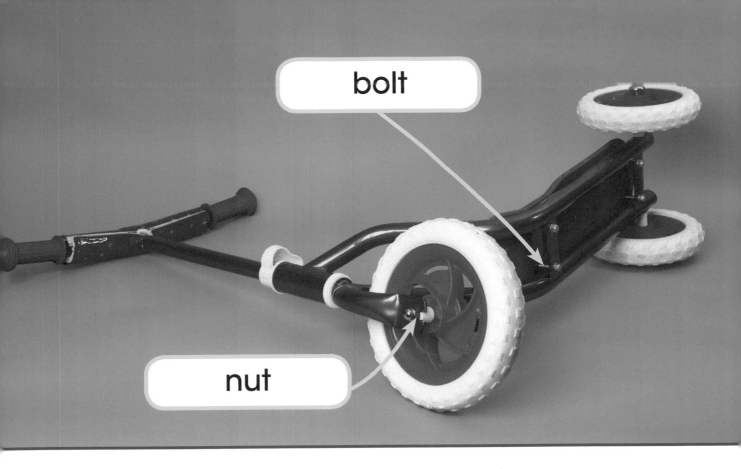

bolt

nut

Nuts and bolts hold this scooter together.

Turning

We have to turn a screw to push it in.

We have to turn a screw to pull it out.

We have to turn a nut to put it on a bolt.

screwdriver

We use a screwdriver to turn a screw.

wrench

We use a wrench to turn a nut.

Quiz

a
b
c
d

Which one of these toys uses screws?

Answer on page 24

Picture Glossary

 **bolt** kind of thick screw with a flat end

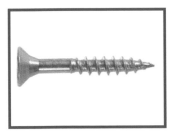 **nut** small piece of metal or plastic with a hole in it

 **screw** thin, pointed piece of metal similar to a nail. A screw has a spiral wrapped around it.

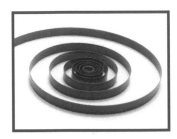 **spiral** shape like a curl that winds around and around

Index

Answer to question on page 22: Toy b uses screws.

Notes for Parents and Teachers

Introduction

Show the children a collection of screws, nails, nuts, and bolts. Select children to pick out a screw, a nail, a nut, and a bolt. Label one example of each. What similarities and differences can they find between the nail, the screw, and the bolt? What do we use these things for?

More information about screws, nuts, and bolts

Explain that screws and bolts are different from nails because they have a spiral (or helix) shape wrapped around the outside. On a screw, this is called the thread. The thread on a screw means that you have to turn the screw to put it in something or take it out. A bolt is like a thicker screw, and most bolts have flat ends. Children can look at the thread on the end of a bolt and the thread inside a nut. They can then see how a nut can be put on a bolt to hold things in place.

Follow-up activities

Give the children the opportunity to experience how screws, nuts, and bolts can be used to hold things together. They could build or take apart models using a construction set. Show them how to use a screwdriver and wrench safely. For more advanced work on simple machines, children can work with an adult to discuss and play the games at: www.edheads.org/activities/simple-machines.